About the Author

ROBERT CECIL, CMG, MA was
Chairman of the Graduate School
of Contemporary European Studies,
University of Reading (1976-8), and
Chairman of the Institute for Cultural
Research, for which he edited an
anthology, *The King's Son* (Octagon
Press, 1980). His other published works
include *Life in Edwardian England*
(1969), *The Myth of the Master Race:
Rosenberg and Nazi Ideology* (1972),
Hitler's Decision to Invade Russia
(1975), *A Divided Life: a biography
of Donald Maclean* (1988), and *The
Masks of Death: Changing Attitudes
in the Nineteenth Century* (1991).

This monograph is the text of a lecture delivered under the aegis of the Institute for Cultural Research.

EDUCATION AND ELITISM IN NAZI GERMANY

Robert Cecil

1971

MONOGRAPH SERIES NO. 5

The Institute for Cultural Research

Education and Elitism in Nazi Germany

IF WE SPEAK of political indoctrination in a particular educational system, we must be clear at the outset that all educational systems embody some degree of indoctrination. All social systems tend to perpetuate themselves and teachers are the product of a particular social system. Even if they try to be objective, they are unlikely to be wholly successful, if only because deeply engrained prejudices often evade the most conscientious self-criticism.

Explore the convictions of a man who declares himself to be non-political and you will usually find in him a staunch upholder of the established social order, which in his mind he has placed beyond the reach of debate. The most subtle and effective indoctrination can be that carried out unconsciously by someone who believes himself to be objective.

At the same time, non-totalitarian systems tend to carry within themselves certain safeguards against rigid uniformity; this is especially true of systems that are decentralised and in which local power of decision plays a role. In the recent controversy in this country about comprehensive schools the real threat to the traditional British educational system lay not in the abolition of Grammar Schools, but in the wish expressed by the Labour

Government to coerce Local Education Authorities. There are two other important safeguards, both of which are observed in this country. One is freedom of research and expression, designed to produce scholars and teachers who are primarily concerned to discover the truth and make it known. The other is the existence of a variety of schools of different kinds; in this country the tradition is of state schools and private schools; in Germany, as in other continental countries, it has been of state schools and religious, or confessional, schools. Whatever the exact character of the built-in safeguards, the best Ministry of Education is that which interferes least in the operation of the system.

It must be clear that, whilst the safeguards mentioned may protect freedom of thought, they will only contribute in an indirect manner to the achievement and maintenance of what are currently regarded as acceptable academic standards. In particular, they will not automatically work towards producing school-leavers who are well fitted in all respects to comply with the political and economic requirements of whatever government is in power. The more concerned that government may be to have at its disposal human material designed to fulfil some military, political or economic purpose, the more the freedom of the system will be at risk. No educational system can remain free if it is regarded primarily as a mechanism for producing citizens of a specific kind needed by the state, whether these be technologists, colonial administrators or merely canon-fodder. The inefficiency of a system to function in the way in which the state wishes it to function may, in certain circumstances, be its best safeguard.

After this cautionary preamble, let us briefly examine the educational system of the Second German Reich – the Reich founded in 1871 – and see how many of the safeguards it embodied. In the first place, it was a federal system; there was no Reich Minister of Education; each of the constituent states had its own Minister, usually known as *Kultusminister*. At the same time it must be remembered that Prussia practised a centralised administrative system and Prussia was two-thirds of the Reich. In the second place, there was a precious tradition of research for its own sake in German Universities – the tradition connected with the name of Humboldt. This had tended to produce two kinds of professors: those who considered that affairs of state were none of their business; and those who considered it to be their duty to uphold the state in every respect. The latter tendency, personified by such men as Treitschke, was further promoted by the fact that the professoriate was part of the civil service; not for nothing was it dubbed in Prussia 'the intellectual bodyguard of the Hohenzollerns'. In Prussian schools the influence of the state was even stronger, because since the time of Frederick the Great the practice had grown up of pensioning off NCOs by appointing them to teach in primary schools. Even in secondary schools the rank of reserve officer was more coveted than any academic distinction. Every effort was made to inculcate into pupils an attitude of undiscriminating loyalty to the King-Emperor.

The best potential safeguard lay in the predominance of confessional schools. In particular the Roman Catholics had become wary of the state in the course of the struggle between Bismarck and the Catholic hierarchy known as the *Kulturkampf*. The same could not be said, however, of the Lutheran Churches which, although organised on the basis of the constituent states of the Reich, recognised the German Emperor as their head. The breaking of this link between throne and altar, which occurred with the abdication of the Kaiser in 1918, was one of the grievances against the Weimar Republic fostered within the ranks of the Protestants.

The educational system was not only sharply divided along religious lines; it also split along class lines. Pupils who went to Grammar Schools, or Gymnasia, as they were called, did eight years of Greek and Latin before passing the school-leaving examination (*Abitur*), which took them to university. There studies were further prolonged partly through the German tradition of frequent movement from one university to another and partly because there was no degree available below that of doctorate or Ph.D. Evidently only the upper class and bourgeoisie could afford to finance so lengthy a period of education before embarking on a career. Towards the end of the nineteenth century this concentration on classical study and research had begun to attract criticism and, as the result of a conference convened by the Kaiser, some modifications were introduced into the curriculum of schools. These only served, however, to make the teaching more nationalistic; more German history, geography and folklore was taught, as well as more physical training with a view to producing fitter reserve officers.

If Prussian Generals, industrialists and civil servants were inclined to think that the system did too little to prepare young people for the realities of the world about them, the students' complaint was against the reality itself. The stern discipline of parents and teachers offended them; they saw little attraction in the life of profit-making or unswerving service to the state for which they were being prepared. Their disenchantment was illustrated by the Wandervogel (bird of passage) movement, which flourished before the First World War. Groups of young people, travelling light – both in terms of baggage and intellectual equipment – wandered through the German woods under leaders distinguished more by charisma than status. They were escapists rather than rebels, living in a shadowy world between an imaginary and heroic Nordic past and a visionary future, which they had read between the lines of Nietzsche and Stefan George. Opposed, as they were on emotional grounds, to urbanisation and industrialisation, they were easily persuaded that these developments were due to Jewish influence, not to the general desire in Germany, as elsewhere, to make higher profits and raise living standards. By 1914, 84% of all Wandervogel groups showed traits of antisemitism. They were the forerunners of the students who in 1933 burnt Heine's books and drove Jewish and liberal-minded teachers out of German universities.

The German Revolution of November 1918, apart from bringing about the disappearance of the Emperor,

Kings and Princes, led to no important changes in the social system. The educational system came in for criticism; on the Left feeling was that more should be taught about the duties of citizenship; the traditional social hierarchy was thought to have failed. The overwhelming impulses, however, were those of intense nationalism, nurtured by bitter resentment against the Treaty of Versailles. As the political and economic situation worsened, the demand grew ever louder for a charismatic leader, who would not content himself with leading young people through the woodlands, but would lead pure-blooded Germans back to a position of honourable equality in Europe, or even to the hegemony that had seemed in 1917 to be within their grasp. More and more Germans sought refuge from the evils of the post-war world in a flight into an unreal world of myth and legend, in which their army had, they claimed, stood undefeated against the foe, but had been betrayed by crafty enemies on the home front, especially the Jews and Marxists.

It was in this atmosphere of unreality that the Nazis began propagating their irrational ideology, preparing men's minds to accept the totalitarian system, which they propounded as the desperate remedy for a situation that no longer seemed tolerable. The Nazis claimed to be a revolutionary Party, but they also claimed to be able to restore Germany's former greatness. They were thus particularly effective in their appeals to the younger generation which, as Fritz Stern has expressed it, was 'conservative out of nostalgia and revolutionary out of despair'. It was not, of course, the immediate past of the Second Reich that they wished to restore – that was a Reich that had failed. It had failed because it had allowed its 'pure Aryan' racial heritage to be defiled by assimilation of Slav and Jewish elements. It had failed because it had ceased to instil belief in the heroic ideals of a remoter epoch. As Alfred Rosenberg put it in his book, *The Myth of the Twentieth Century*, 'The Germany of the bourgeoisie and the Marxists was without a myth; Germany no longer had a supreme value in which it believed, for which it was ready to fight.' In his view the Nazis' most vital task, in the long run, was to evolve an Aryan type, which would conserve the purity of his blood (*Blut*) and fight to defend its soil (*Boden*). Above all, it would be hard and ruthless in carrying out the commands of its chosen leader.

Hannah Arendt has written, 'Total power can be achieved and safeguarded only in a world of conditioned reflexes.' This was not, of course, what the Nazis said, but it was the principle on which they acted.

What they said was that the true Aryans were a Master Race (*Herrenvolk*), whose heroic leaders were the incarnation of Nietzsche's ideal of the Superman (*Uebermensch*); the fact that Nietzsche had meant no such thing did not at all trouble them. To many Germans, living precariously in a defeated country, which after 1929 was again close to bankruptcy, this heady doctrine had a strong appeal. As Rosenberg put it, 'Suddenly millions grasped what their task was, one which had been partly forgotten and partly neglected: to live out the myth and create the type.' If this could be achieved, not only would the German people be strong and secure against attack, from without or within, but the Nazis would have ensured the perpetuation of their totalitarian system; the 'Thousand-year Reich' would have come into being. For those who were not attracted by this vision of the future, there would be the coercion of the SS and Gestapo and finally, for the recalcitrant, extinction in the concentration camp.

Nazis who concerned themselves with education and indoctrination saw before them three main tasks. First, it was necessary to break down the safeguards still preserving some elements of freedom within the existing educational system. Secondly, it was necessary to breed the new type of citizen – a collective type with a hard outer shell and a soft centre of obedience and personal insecurity;

the new German was to be arrogant towards non-Germans, but submissive towards his own leadership. Thirdly, it was necessary to create an elite, chosen from within the new type, to take over in due course from the present Nazi leadership, whilst preserving rigid uniformity with its ideological conceptions. Although the Nazis made a good deal of play with slogans about the 'community of the people' (*Volksgemeinschaft*), equality in all its aspects was abhorrent to them; the distance between Aryans and inferior races was scarcely greater, in Nazi eyes, than that between the leadership group and the rest of the German people. The selection and training of the elite was particularly important, because the Nazis lacked any theory, however rudimentary, about the nature of the state. Hitler had declined to replace

Hindenburg as President; he had simply become 'Fuehrer', a designation unknown to constitutional lawyers. No means existed, other than exercise of the Fuehrer's will, for choosing his successor. Although he ruled by decree, he had never troubled to rescind the Weimar constitution or adopt another; by 1938 even the Cabinet had ceased to meet. No machinery of Government interfered with the freedom of the Fuehrer and his henchman, especially the SS, to rule as they pleased. Their only problem was how to perpetuate their power.

It did not take the Nazis very long to reshape the educational system. Private schools – never very numerous in Germany – were soon brought under control or eliminated altogether, as in the case of Salem, founded by Kurt Hahn, who emigrated to

Britain. In 1933, when Hitler came to power, 83% of all public elementary schools were confessional; as a first step, the Nazis began to exclude priests and Protestant pastors from giving religious instruction; then such teaching was gradually crowded out of the curriculum. By 1938-39 the influence of the Churches on the schools had largely been eliminated, in spite of a Concordat drawn up in 1933 between the Vatican and Hitler, designed to protect the rights of the Roman Catholic Church. Youth movements in Germany had also been organised along confessional lines. The Protestants voluntarily merged their organisations in the Hitler Youth (HJ) in his first year of power. The Catholics held out longer, protected by the Concordat, but by the end of 1936 their youth movements, too, had been absorbed by the HJ. 'The Youth belongs to us!' Goebbels claimed; the Nazis had no intention of sharing their control over young minds at the impressionable age.

The Nazis were equally forthright in measures to centralise the educational system and abolish academic freedom in the universities. In January 1934 the various Kultusministers were subordinated to the Reich Minister of the Interior; then four months later the Prussian Kultusminister, Bernhard Rust, who had been a school-teacher and an ardent Nazi, became Reich Minister of Education. A Central Institute of Education was set up under another Nazi, Rudolf Benze, who defined education as 'the directing of growth'. By 1939 all teachers, who had been officials of the state (*Land*) governments, became officials of the

Reich. In the following year special teacher training institutions were created, in which candidates had to submit to ideological tests and undergo training to become youth leaders in the HJ. Addressing a group of teachers on one occasion, Rosenberg made no secret of what was expected of them: 'The National-Socialist ideology claims its rights over the whole human being, and you in your schools and affiliations will have this human being, beginning with his unripe years and lasting to the grave.' No evasion of Nazi domination over the minds of its citizens was to be permitted.

As regards academic freedom at universities, the task of the Nazis was made very much easier by reactionary students, who by 1931-32 (i.e. before Hitler came to power) had taken over representative student bodies in all but a few Catholic universities. They were ready to burn books to order and make life unbearable for Jewish and other professors, who had fallen foul of the Nazi regime. Where these tactics did not at once succeed, the Nazis stepped in and imposed Vice-Chancellors (*Rektors*) on whom they could rely. Some Rektors needed no persuasion; the existentialist philosopher, Heidegger, in his inaugural address at Freiburg, insisted that academic freedom now meant to serve the community of the people in the Labour Service (*Arbeitsdienst*), the Fatherland in conscription and the intellectual needs of the people in science. The fact that conscription was banned by the Treaty of Versailles and by German law did not in any way trouble him.

It can be no surprise that, in such circumstances, the objectivity of research, on which Germans had rightly prided themselves, suffered crippling blows. Perhaps the worst feature was the virtual abandonment in some areas of the inductive method, on which the entire structure of scientific thought had been developed since the Middle Ages. It was no longer a question of assembling facts before forming a working hypothesis; it was necessary, in order to pursue research and get it published, to accept in advance certain dogmatic assumptions about biological laws, transmission of hereditary characteristics, features of Germanic prehistory and the like. Nazi ideology embodied vulgarisation of theories about evolution and survival, growth of population and heredity, which had been tentatively put forward in the nineteenth century by Darwin, Malthus, Mendel and others.

The task of academics was simply to provide illustrations of these crude theories, as understood by the Nazis. It was assumed that, through genetics and what was called 'racial hygiene', it would be possible to breed a type of Superman, just as it was possible by breeding to produce a swift-moving greyhound or horse. Men like Himmler and Darre had no difficulty in regarding themselves as privy to the mysterious purposes of creation. Prohibition of mixed marriages for Aryans, sterilisation of non-Aryans and euthanasia for the incurable represented only a part of the means advocated.

Outside the universities, other techniques were introduced to promote indoctrination of the young. All subjects of study were permeated with militarism; sport was to instil discipline and endurance; geography was to promote map-reading; arithmetic was to help range-finding; chemistry was related to producing explosives. Nothing was studied for its own sake. School or party uniform was to be worn on every occasion to encourage the idea that the individual had no existence apart from the organised group to which he belonged. To discourage thought, the groups formed ranks and marched everywhere. Rosenberg described the new German style: 'It is the style of a marching column, no matter where or to what end this column may be marching.' Theirs not to reason why had been elevated to an educational principle. In the same spirit the Nazis introduced what is today known in some Communist countries as polytechnic education; that is to say, pupils in special secondary schools (of which more shortly) had to spend some weeks working on the land or in a factory. Students before going to university had to pass through the Labour Service; in addition, conscription was brought back in 1935.

One of the most effective techniques of indoctrination was to take young men away from their parents and familiar surroundings and put them in a camp or under canvas for a few weeks. There the individual was exposed to the full pressure of mass-made opinion; mockery or rough horse-play soon weeded out or coerced those who were not at first disposed to conform. At first tents or hutments were used because the Nazis were improvising; the provisional character remained because discomfort was part of the indoctrination process and impermanence stressed the insignificance of the individual. By contrast, Berlin, Munich and other cities boasted the monstrous neo-classical buildings, designed by Speer, the Fuehrer's architect, and others to house the leadership and emphasise the all-powerful functions of government. To quote Rosenberg again, 'Monumental buildings are not houses, but the ideas in stone of a community.'

When we come to discuss the formation of elite cadres, we must begin by ridding ourselves of the idea that Nazi totalitarianism was as monolithic as the Stalinist variety. A leader who had once secured his foothold in the hierarchy, provided that he observed the Fuehrer's dictates in priority matters, was able to carve out a semi-autonomous satrapy for himself and even indulge in political in-fighting with colleagues and competitors in the struggle for power within the state. This led, among other things, to two distinct concepts of elitism. The better known is Himmler's SS, which began as the Fuehrer's bodyguard, took over the security functions of party and state, and ended by forming a private army-cum-police force, which interpenetrated public and, indeed, personal life. Although the SS was universally feared, its claim to be the elite of the party, and thus of the nation, was never generally recognised, even within the party itself. Even for some Nazi minds, the contradiction was too crass between the concept of an elite and the role of paid spy, informer and guardian of concentration camps. Rival elitist claims were accordingly promoted, on behalf of the party as a whole, by Robert Ley, who was in charge of party organisation, and Baldur v. Schirach, who headed the HJ.

In 1937 Ley and Schirach instituted the Adolf Hitler schools, which were outside the state educational system and financed from party funds. In taking this step, they turned their back upon the initiative taken in 1933 by Rust, the new Prussian Kultusminister, who had created, with a similar aim in view, the special schools known as National Political Educational Institutions (*NAPOLA*). He had not been strong enough, however, to resist the encroachment of the SS, which by 1936 had secured virtual control over the NAPOLA. Candidate-pupils for the Adolf Hitler schools were tested not by the SS but by the HJ and the Nazi regional bosses (*Gauleiter*). Tests were mainly concerned with the physical fitness of candidates and the political reliability and Aryan ancestry of their parents. After less than eighteen months of this method of selection, steps had to be taken to achieve a higher standard of intelligence; even the Nazis began to see that the future of the movement could not be safely entrusted to brainless blonde toughs. Education was ostensibly free in these schools, but parents were expected to contribute generously to Nazi 'charitable' funds. Polytechnic practice applied both in the NAPOLA and in the Adolf Hitler schools.

The Nazis, in their contempt for traditional education, did not intend that the universities should play any significant part in training the elite. Even before the Adolf Hitler schools had come into existence, Ley, Schirach and Rosenberg had cooperated in setting up further education colleges, known as Castles of the Order (*Ordensburgen*) to recall the mission of the Teutonic Order of Knighthood among the heathen Slavs along the shores of the Baltic in the middle ages. Candidates for the four Ordensburgen, in addition to requirements similar to those for the Adolf Hitler schools, had to be twenty-five years of age and to have qualified for a profession, as well as performing military service since leaving school. During their three and a half years at the Ordensburg, they also had practical experience of work for the party; the Ordensburg therefore served the purpose of a staff college, as well as a university. The emphasis on physical fitness and practical experience further aggravated the problem of attaining adequate academic standards; but on one point, at least, the Nazi leaders could be satisfied with their selective process – a striking uniformity prevailed. Ley greeted the first intake of students with these words: 'When I look at you, my men, I know that the principles by which we mustered you are right. Externally you already look alike and in a short time you will be alike inside as well.'

Hitler, musing in the bunker beneath the ruins of Berlin at the end of the lost war, observed to his entourage, 'We lacked men moulded in the shape of our ideal.' To this statement we can only add, 'Thank God.' Yet all that Hitler had lacked was time; he had been in too much of a hurry to conquer and put all to the test, before the long-range plans of breeding the new type of totalitarian man had come to fruition. With a little more patience he might well have succeeded; as it was, resistance to his rule inside Germany was ineffective; resistance to the Allies invading Germany was far more stubborn than in 1918 and, here and there, especially among the SS, it was fanatical. This is a sombre thought, when we also bear in mind that Hitler was only in power for twelve years and that the schools named after him existed for only eight. Since 1945 techniques of indoctrination have become more subtle and development of the mass media has enabled propaganda to be put out on a scale that would arouse the envy of Goebbels. We cannot afford to assume that it is only under totalitarian regimes that such techniques will today be applied; no country can dare to neglect the safeguards that make for freedom within its educational system.

The potentialities of totalitarian man and his mob-mind are inside us all.

(Author's note: Some of the foregoing is embodied in a chapter of Mr Cecil's book, *Alfred Rosenberg and Nazi Ideology*, published by Batsford in 1972).

About Idries Shah

BORN IN 1924 into an aristocratic Afghan family, Idries Shah created a large body of literary work, most of which considered elements of "Eastern Thought", especially Sufism and Sufi thought. Some of his best known works include The Sufis and several collections of teaching stories featuring Nasrudin.

Shah devoted his life to collecting, selecting and translating Sufi books and key works of Sufi classical literature, adapting them to the needs of the West and disseminating them in the Occident.

Called by some "practical philosophy", by others "templates in straight thinking" – these works represent centuries of Sufi thought and Islamic thought aimed at the development of human potential to its fullest extent.

They stress virtues such as commonsense, clear-thinking and humor to counter cant and religious dogma. As such they are vital works in the area of Islamic philosophy, and may be viewed as an antidote to radicalism and fanaticism much needed in the world today.

Shah's books have been translated into dozens of languages, have sold in their millions, and are regarded as a cultural bridge between West and East. His work and contribution to Sufism are represented by The Idries Shah Foundation.

About ISF

ISF IS DEVOTED to championing a sense of imagination, and to teaching stories – the kind of which are contained in the large published corpus of the writer and thinker, Idries Shah.

Engaged in a wide range of charitable projects on a world-wide basis, the Foundation seeks to stimulate the minds of both young and old by regarding the world in new ways.

In collaboration with UNESCO, ISF has begun a major story-writing competition for children in five languages and 180 countries. Other projects are working to give illustrated books to kids in Afghanistan and other conflict zones on a mass scale, thereby sparking the innate sense of imagination in young minds.

Yet another endeavour is striving to build the first global StoryBank – bridging disparate societies through stories – which we regard as the essence of all culture.

Thank you for your support of ISF, and your interest in our projects.

**A list of all the monographs
to be published in the series:**

An Eye to the Future
Dr. Alexander King, Dr. Martin Holdgate, Eugene Grebenik, Dr. Kenneth Mellanby, George McRobie

East and West, Today and Yesterday
Sir Stephen Runciman, Patrick O'Donovan, Peter Brent, Sir Roger Stevens, Nirad C. Chaudhuri, Iris Butler, Prof. G.M. Carstairs, Richard Harris

Science and the Paranormal
Leonard Lewin, D.Sc.

Sufic Traces in Georgian Literature
Katharine Vivian

Rembrandt and Angels
Michael Rubinstein

Biological and Cultural Evolution
Mary Midgley

The Age of Anxiety: a Reassessment
Malcolm Lader

Goethe's Scientific Consciousnes
Henri Bortoft

The Healing Within: Medicine, Health and Wholeness
Robin Price

A Clash of Cultures: The Malaysian Experience
David Widdicombe, Q.C.

Evaluating Spiritual and Utopian Groups
Arthur J. Deikman, M.D.

The Crusades as Connection: Cultural transfer
during the Holy Wars
Contributed by Cultural Research Services

Baptised Sultans: The contribution of Frederick II
of Sicily in the transfer and adaptation of Oriental
ideas to the West
Contributed by Cultural Research Services

Brain Development During Adolescence and
Beyond
Dr. Sarah-Jayne Blakemore

Collective Behaviour and the Physics of Society
Philip Ball

Counter-Intuition
Dr. Kevin Byron

Music, Pleasure and the Brain
Dr. Harry Witchel

Fields of the Mind
Dr. Rupert Sheldrake

Why do we leave it so late?
David Canter

Scheherazade and the global mutation of teaching
stories
Robert Irwin

Consciousness, will and responsibility
Chris Frith

Extraordinary Voyages of the Panchatantra
Ramsay Wood